THE INVISIBLE MOMENTS OF HOSTING

How Trust Is Built Before, During, and After the Stay

Olaf Kohrsmeyer

First edition.

For more information, visit:

www.visiblepr.com

Table of Contents

Introduction

Why This Book Exists

This book wasn't written because hosting is difficult.

It was written because hosting has become noisy.

There is no shortage of advice on pricing, automation, optimization, and growth. Much of it is useful. And yet many hosts still feel that something is off. Bookings come in, but not always the right ones. Reviews are positive, but not always easy. And the work itself can feel heavier than expected — even when things appear to be "working."

This book starts from a different place.

It assumes that most hosts already care. That they clean thoroughly, respond responsibly, and genuinely want guests to have a good stay. It assumes that problems rarely come from a lack of effort, but from misalignment — between what guests expect, what hosts intend, and what actually happens in between.

At its core, hosting is not a marketing problem.

It's a trust problem.

Guests don't book listings. They book a feeling — a sense that things will go smoothly, that the place will be as described, and that the host will be reasonable if something unexpected happens. Most of that decision is made quietly, long before arrival, and often before a message is ever sent.

And yet, very little guidance exists on how that trust is actually formed.

Instead, hosts are taught what to optimize, what to automate, and what to fix — without understanding why certain stays feel calm, why some guests feel immediately aligned, and why others arrive already on edge.

I didn't arrive at these ideas through consulting or theory. I arrived at them the same way most hosts do — by paying attention. By noticing which stays felt calm, which guests felt aligned, and which small details consistently made a difference. Over time, patterns began to emerge. This book is a reflection of those patterns, observed from the inside.

This is not a guide to platforms, tools, or tactics.

It doesn't promise quick wins or clever shortcuts. Those things change too quickly to matter for long.

What doesn't change is how people decide.

This book looks at hosting through the lens of the guest journey — before the booking, during the stay, and after checkout — and explores how trust is built quietly, through small, often overlooked signals. It focuses on clarity instead of persuasion, consistency instead of perfection, and presence instead of performance.

You won't find checklists here.

You'll find explanations.

The goal is not to tell you what to do, but to help you understand why certain things work — so your decisions feel steadier and less reactive. When hosts understand the dynamics of trust, many of the right choices begin to make sense on their own.

This book is written for hosts who care about longevity.

For those who don't want to host louder, but better.

For those who value fewer problems over more bookings, and alignment over optimization.

If you're looking for quick results, this book may feel slow.

If you're looking for a system that compounds quietly over time, you're in the right place.

We begin before the booking —

in the moment you never see.

1 The Moment You Never See

Most hosts never see the moment a guest almost books — and then doesn't.

There is no notification for hesitation. No message that says, *"I liked your place, but something didn't feel clear enough."* From the host's side, everything looks quiet and normal. The calendar doesn't change. No inquiry arrives. No feedback is given. But on the guest's side, a decision is already unfolding — slowly, quietly, and mostly invisibly.

This is not a failure of the listing.

It's not a mistake.

It's simply how people make decisions when money, uncertainty, and emotion intersect.

Booking a stay is a risk decision disguised as a transaction. Guests are committing to a place they've never been, hosted by someone they don't know, often in a location they don't fully understand yet. Even when a listing looks good, the question is rarely *"Is this a nice place?"* The real question is subtler:

"Will this go smoothly?"

That question is almost never asked out loud.

Guests don't want to negotiate reassurance. They don't want to feel difficult, needy, or unsure. Instead, they scan, compare, and sense. They look for signs that others have gone before them and that nothing unexpected awaits. When those signs are present, booking feels easy. When they aren't, guests don't argue with themselves — they simply keep looking.

This is why many listings that are objectively good still lose bookings.

Most guests don't read listings carefully. They scan them. They scroll quickly, pause briefly, and move on. Their eyes look for patterns: familiar layouts, consistent photos, calm language, predictable structure. This happens subconsciously. Guests are not analyzing your listing — they are feeling their way through it.

Confusion rarely feels like confusion.

It feels like hesitation.

A missing photo doesn't register as "missing." It registers as a small pause. An overly enthusiastic description doesn't feel wrong — it feels slightly uncertain. A rule explained too defensively doesn't feel informative — it feels like a warning. None of these things are deal breakers on their own. But together, they add friction to a decision that already carries risk.

At this stage, guests are not trying to find reasons to book.

They are trying to eliminate reasons not to.

There are a few silent questions most guests carry with them as they browse. They almost never send these questions as messages, but they are always present:

Is this place real?

Will the experience match the photos?

Is the host reasonable and responsive?

Are there any surprises I'll discover too late?

Will I regret choosing this over another option?

Every unanswered question increases friction — not dramatically, but enough.

When friction appears, guests don't usually ask for clarification. They move on. Silence, from the host's perspective, often looks like neutrality. From the guest's perspective, it is a decision already made.

This is why response rates, pricing strategies, and availability calendars only tell part of the story. Long before any message is sent, guests are already deciding how safe a booking feels. That decision happens privately, quickly, and emotionally.

When trust isn't completed in one place, people naturally look for it somewhere else.

Sometimes that means reading reviews more carefully. Sometimes it means searching the location. Sometimes it means leaving the platform entirely for a moment — not to investigate deeply, but to confirm a feeling. Guests are not trying to uncover secrets. They are trying to reassure themselves that the experience will be as straightforward as it appears.

Most great hosts don't lose bookings because they did something wrong.

They lose them because they never realized what guests needed before they were ready to ask.

This book is about understanding that invisible moment — and quietly supporting it.

Not with tricks or tactics, but with clarity, consistency, and a system that works with how people actually decide.

2 Listings Are Scanned, Not Read

Most hosts believe guests read listings.

They don't.

Guests scroll. They pause. They skim. Their eyes move faster than their thoughts, and decisions form before words are fully processed. This isn't carelessness — it's efficiency. Faced with dozens of similar options, guests reduce complexity the only way the brain knows how: by scanning for signals.

Understanding this changes everything.

When guests scan a listing, they aren't trying to understand it fully. They're trying to answer one question quickly:

"Does this feel clear and predictable?"

If the answer is yes, they slow down.

If the answer is no — even slightly — they move on.

This happens far more often than hosts realize.

Listings are designed for speed. Platforms encourage concise descriptions, bullet points, and visual emphasis. That's not a flaw; it reflects how people browse. But it also means clarity matters more than completeness. Guests rarely absorb every detail. Instead, they look for patterns that tell them whether reading further is worth their attention.

Those patterns are subtle.

A calm headline.

Photos that feel consistent.

Language that sounds measured rather than promotional.

Rules that feel informative instead of defensive.

Guests may not consciously register these elements, but they feel their absence immediately.

This is why adding more information doesn't always improve a listing. More words can increase noise. More enthusiasm can raise questions. More explanation can feel like justification. When too much is happening at once, guests don't think *"This host is thorough."* They think *"This feels like work."*

Confusion rarely announces itself clearly.

It shows up as hesitation.

A description that tries too hard to impress can feel less trustworthy than one that simply explains. A listing that overemphasizes uniqueness can accidentally raise the question of what's being compensated for. None of this is intentional — and none of it is dishonest — but perception doesn't operate on intention.

Guests scan for ease.

They look for signs that the experience will be straightforward. That nothing needs to be decoded. That expectations are aligned before arrival. When listings feel simple and well-structured, guests relax. When they feel cluttered or emotionally charged, guests brace themselves — often without knowing why.

This scanning behavior also explains why guests sometimes ask questions that are already answered in the listing. It's not because the information is missing. It's because it didn't register during the scan. The brain filtered it out as secondary.

Hosts often interpret these questions as inattention. In reality, they are a signal: something about the listing didn't settle fully.

Clarity is not about saying everything.

It's about making the important things easy to recognize.

When guests scan a listing and feel oriented, they move forward. When they don't, they keep browsing — not because the place wasn't good enough, but because the decision didn't feel resolved quickly enough.

This isn't a call to simplify hosting.

It's a call to respect how decisions are actually made.

Once hosts accept that listings are scanned, not read, they stop trying to convince and start trying to clarify. And clarity, more than persuasion, is what allows guests to feel safe moving closer to a decision.

The next question, of course, is what guests rely on when scanning isn't enough — and why images often carry more weight than words ever could.

That's where we turn next.

3 Photos as Proof, Not Decoration

Most guests don't trust descriptions on their own.

They may read them — or skim them — but images do more of the deciding. Photos are where trust either settles or remains incomplete. They function less as decoration and more as proof.

This is because guests aren't looking for beauty.

They're looking for confirmation.

When someone considers a place they've never been, hosted by someone they don't know, photos answer questions words cannot. They show scale. Light. Context. Condition. They reveal whether the space feels honest.

Perfect images don't necessarily help.

Highly staged photos can impress, but they can also raise suspicion. When everything looks curated to the point of abstraction, guests start wondering what's missing. Real images, even when imperfect, tend to feel more trustworthy because they resemble how people actually experience spaces.

This doesn't mean careless photography.

It means intentional realism.

Photos that show how rooms relate to each other. How light moves through the space. How furniture is actually arranged.

How the surroundings feel beyond the frame of a single hero shot. These details reduce uncertainty.

Guests are not analyzing photos consciously.

They are sensing whether the space feels stable. Whether it looks easy to inhabit. Whether what they see aligns with what they imagine arriving to.

This is why image consistency matters more than image quality alone.

A mix of styles, lighting conditions, or visual moods can create subtle doubt. Guests may not articulate it, but they feel the inconsistency. When images feel coherent, guests relax. They stop scanning for red flags and start imagining themselves there.

Photos also carry responsibility.

If an image suggests an experience the stay doesn't fully deliver, disappointment follows — even if nothing is technically wrong. The issue isn't that expectations were too high. It's that they were misaligned.

Good photos don't promise more.

They promise accurately.

They show what guests will find, not what they could be sold. When reality meets expectation cleanly, trust deepens. When it doesn't, guests become more critical — not because the place is bad, but because the signal was off.

This is why photos reduce perceived risk.

They close the gap between imagination and reality before arrival. They allow guests to settle into the idea of the stay early. And when guests feel settled, they move forward more confidently.

Words can clarify.

Photos convince.

And when the two work together, guests stop questioning and start deciding.

4 When Guests Leave the Platform

When scanning isn't enough, guests leave.

Not dramatically. Not with suspicion or intent. They don't think, *"I don't trust this listing."* They think, *"Let me just check one more thing."* And with that, they step outside the platform — quietly, briefly, and often without realizing how decisive that moment is.

This behavior surprises many hosts, but it shouldn't.

Guests don't leave platforms because something is wrong. They leave because something is unresolved. The listing answered most of their questions, but not all of them. And when a decision involves money, time, and expectation, the mind looks for reassurance wherever it can find it.

This is not comparison shopping.

It's confirmation.

Guests may search the location to better understand the area. They may look for images that feel less curated. They may try to understand who the host is beyond a profile photo and a few sentences. None of this is driven by distrust. It's driven by the desire to feel oriented before committing.

Importantly, guests don't expect to find much.

They aren't looking for hidden information or deeper detail. They're looking for consistency. They want to see the same tone repeated elsewhere. The same calm. The same sense that nothing is being withheld. When they find that, they return to the platform with greater confidence. When they don't, hesitation lingers — sometimes without knowing why.

Silence outside the platform can feel louder than intended.

When guests find nothing, they don't assume the worst. But they do notice the absence. A lack of external presence doesn't signal dishonesty — it signals incompleteness. And incompleteness creates just enough friction to make another option feel easier.

This is especially true for guests who are already cautious by nature.

Not every guest leaves the platform. But those who do are often the ones who care most about predictability, alignment, and smooth experiences. These are not difficult guests. They are thoughtful ones. And when their need for reassurance isn't met, they quietly self-select out.

What guests find outside the platform matters less than how it feels.

They aren't evaluating design quality or brand polish. They are sensing tone. They are asking themselves whether what they see elsewhere matches what they've already imagined. If the story continues without contradiction, trust compounds. If it fragments, doubt reappears.

This is why trust cannot live in one place alone.

A listing may be clear, photos may be honest, and reviews may be positive — but if these elements don't echo beyond the platform, the guest's mental picture remains unfinished. People are remarkably good at detecting when something feels only partially formed.

Hosts rarely know when this happens.

There is no alert that says a guest searched for you. No indication that they paused to confirm. No feedback when that confirmation wasn't found. From the host's perspective, it simply looks like another guest who didn't book.

But from the guest's perspective, this moment often decides whether they return — reassured — or move on.

When trust needs more space than a platform can provide, guests naturally look for it elsewhere. What they find doesn't need to be impressive. It needs to be consistent. Quiet. Familiar.

The places that understand this don't try to control the search. They simply make sure that wherever a guest briefly lands, the same story continues.

That's when reassurance stops feeling like something that has to be earned — and starts feeling like something that's already present.

5 The Connected Presence

Guests don't experience your place in one place.

They may first see it on Airbnb. They may later encounter it through a Google search, a map result, a social post, or a link shared by the host. Sometimes this happens before booking. Often it happens after. Rarely does it happen in a planned or linear way.

What matters is not where guests arrive — but how consistent the experience feels when they do.

From the guest's perspective, these touchpoints blend together. They are not evaluated as separate platforms. They are felt as one presence. One host. One tone. When that presence feels coherent, trust builds quietly. When it doesn't, friction appears — even if everything looks fine on its own.

This is why trust cannot live in a single listing.

An Airbnb listing is designed for clarity. It answers practical questions, sets expectations, and allows guests to make a decision efficiently. That's exactly what it should do. But by design, it cannot carry the full emotional surface of a stay. It compresses experience into facts, photos, and structure.

Other platforms do the same in different ways.

A search result offers legitimacy.

A map listing offers orientation.

A social post offers a glimpse.

Each one shows a fragment.

Most hosts today maintain a simple website alongside their listing. Not as a replacement for Airbnb, and not as a separate booking channel, but as a stable point of reference they fully control. Unlike listings, search results, or social platforms, a website isn't compressed by format or driven by algorithms. It allows tone, language, and intention to exist in one place, unchanged.

Its role is not to replace any other platform guests may encounter.

Its role is to **hold the center** — so that wherever guests briefly arrive, what they see feels consistent, familiar, and clearly connected to the same host.

A good website acts as a reference point — not because guests spend a long time there, but because it establishes tone, language, and intention in one place. Wherever guests encounter you elsewhere, what they see should feel like it comes from the same source.

This is not about branding in the traditional sense.

It's about coherence.

When the tone of your listing, your messages, your website, and any external presence feel aligned, guests stop recalibrating. They don't need to adjust expectations as they move between platforms. Nothing contradicts what they already believe. That absence of contradiction is what allows trust to settle.

Importantly, the website does not try to pull guests away from Airbnb.

It doesn't compete with the platform.

It doesn't promise a different booking path.

It doesn't ask guests to choose.

When a booking option appears on the website, it leads directly back to Airbnb. The decision stays where it belongs. The website exists to support the booking — not intercept it.

This distinction matters.

Guests don't want to manage multiple processes. They don't want to wonder where the "real" booking happens. When the website clearly reinforces Airbnb as the point of transaction, professionalism increases. The experience feels organized, not fragmented.

Because the website is not tied to a single moment in the journey, guests may arrive there at different times.

Some arrive before booking, looking for reassurance.

Many arrive after booking, through a link shared by the host.

Some return later, simply to reconnect with the place they chose.

In every case, the purpose remains the same: to confirm that the experience feels whole.

A connected presence doesn't ask for attention.

It reduces friction by feeling familiar wherever it appears.

When everything points back to the same center — the same tone, the same calm, the same clarity — guests don't think about trust at all.

They simply feel that they're in good hands.

6 After the Booking

Reassurance and Anticipation

Most guests don't know you have a website.

They didn't discover it while browsing, and they didn't go looking for it on their own. For most bookings, the website enters the story only after the decision is already made — when the guest has booked and the initial relief of securing a place is followed by a quieter question:

"What happens now?"

This moment matters more than it appears.

After booking, guests briefly revisit their decision. Not because they regret it, but because commitment creates awareness. The stay is no longer abstract. It's real. And with that comes a natural desire for reassurance — and, just as often, anticipation.

This is where many thoughtful hosts intentionally introduce the website.

Usually, it's done simply. A confirmation message. A thank-you. And a line that reframes what the link is for:

"We've put together a small website about the place and the area — just so you can get a feel for what's ahead."

That language matters.

It doesn't suggest obligation.

It doesn't imply missing information.

It doesn't redirect the booking.

It frames the website as a gesture, not a requirement.

When guests click the link at this stage, they aren't deciding anymore. They're settling into an experience they've already chosen. And what they find there has a very specific effect.

First, reassurance.

A professional, coherent website confirms that the stay is well managed. That the host is organized. That the experience has been considered beyond the listing. Guests don't consciously analyze this — but background anxiety lowers. They ask fewer logistical questions. They worry less about surprises.

Second, orientation.

The website quietly answers questions guests haven't asked yet. How the place is situated. What the surroundings feel like. How the rhythm of the stay might unfold. This doesn't overwhelm them with detail — it simply gives their imagination somewhere concrete to land.

Third, anticipation.

Unlike an Airbnb listing, the website doesn't need to stay strictly factual. It can include lifestyle images, light context about the area, and a sense of pace that wouldn't belong on the platform itself. This isn't about selling the stay — it's about allowing guests to look forward to it.

This combination matters.

When reassurance and anticipation arrive together, guests settle faster. They feel more confident about their choice and more connected to what's ahead. The stay begins emotionally earlier — and that has practical consequences.

Guests who feel settled cancel less.

They arrive calmer.

They interpret small imperfections more generously.

Not because expectations were raised, but because confidence was.

Importantly, the website does not replace communication.

It supports it.

It gives guests a place to return to between booking and arrival — a quiet anchor that holds the experience steady while time passes. Even guests who only glance at it benefit from knowing it exists.

This is the shift that happens after booking.

The decision phase ends.

The experience phase begins — first in imagination, and soon after in reality.

And by the time guests arrive, they don't feel like they're stepping into something unknown. They feel like they're arriving somewhere they already recognize.

That's when hosting stops being about reassurance —

and becomes about delivery.

7 Arrival Is the First Review

By the time guests arrive, the review has already begun.

Not in words, but in feeling. The expectations they carry — shaped by the listing, the messages, and the reassurance after booking — meet reality in the first few minutes. That meeting is decisive. Long before a bed is tested or a shower is used, guests begin forming the impression they will later describe as *"everything was exactly as expected"* — or not.

Arrival is not a single moment.

It's a sequence.

And that sequence begins before guests ever reach the door.

A few days before arrival, there is often a quiet gap. The booking is complete. The stay is approaching. But nothing is happening yet. For guests, this space can feel either calm — or oddly empty.

This is where a short, well-timed message does important work.

Not to provide instructions.

Not to overwhelm.

But to signal readiness.

A brief note sent two or three days before arrival reassures guests that the host is present, prepared, and expecting them. It closes the silence without opening complexity.

A message at this stage might include only a few elements:

A warm confirmation that the host is looking forward to the stay.

A simple link to the location, so guests can orient themselves.

A note that full arrival instructions will be shared on the day of arrival for convenience.

The clarity here matters.

Guests don't want to manage information too early. They want to know it will arrive at the right time. When hosts signal that timing intentionally, trust increases.

This message can also gently open space for anticipation.

If the host offers optional add-ons or experiences, this is the moment to reference them — not as a sales pitch, but as an invitation. A simple line such as *"If you'd like to take a look at a few optional experiences we offer, you can find them here"* keeps the tone light and optional.

When add-ons are offered, they work best when they live on a separate page of the website — not mixed into arrival details or messages. This keeps information clean and optional. The purpose of that page is not to push an upgrade, but to give guests a sense of what's possible during their stay. When guests choose to add something, payment is still handled through Airbnb, just like the booking itself. This keeps the process familiar, secure, and clearly connected — and reassures guests that both platforms are working together, not competing.

Guests who are interested explore.

Guests who aren't feel no pressure.

Importantly, this pre-arrival message should not include access details.

Arrival instructions belong to the day of arrival — when guests are ready to act on them. Separating reassurance from instruction prevents confusion and keeps the experience orderly.

The final role of this message is subtle but powerful: preparation.

Asking for an estimated arrival time, framed correctly, reassures guests that the space will be ready for them specifically. Language matters here. The question is not about monitoring — it's about care.

A simple note such as *"If you have a rough idea of your arrival time, feel free to share it so we can make sure everything is perfectly prepared"* signals intention without pressure.

By the time guests arrive, the emotional groundwork has already been laid.

Arrival itself then unfolds in sequence.

When guests approach the property.

When they find the entrance.

When they unlock the door.

When they step inside and take in the space without explanation.

Each transition either confirms what they already believe — or introduces friction.

This is why arrival matters more than hosts often realize.

Guests are not looking to be impressed. They are looking for confirmation. They want the place to feel familiar — not because they've been there before, but because nothing contradicts what they imagined. When the first minutes feel smooth, the rest of the stay unfolds more generously.

Clarity does most of the work here.

Clear directions.

Clear access.

Clear expectations about arrival itself.

When guests don't have to ask questions immediately, they relax. When they do, they begin managing the experience instead of receiving it.

Importantly, arrival is not the time to explain everything.

Guests need space to orient themselves. Too much information too soon creates noise. What reassures most is the sense that help is available — not that it must be used.

This is where earlier reassurance pays off.

Guests who arrive already confident interpret small uncertainties more generously. They assume good intent. They trust that anything unexpected will be handled reasonably. The emotional work has already been done.

Guests who arrive uncertain do the opposite. They notice friction faster. They interpret ambiguity defensively — not because they are difficult, but because the foundation wasn't fully settled.

Arrival sets that foundation.

It is the point where trust stops being theoretical and becomes experiential. Where anticipation meets reality. Where the tone of the stay is quietly established.

When arrival feels smooth, guests stop assessing and start living. They unpack. They settle in. They breathe differently.

The stay begins.

And from that moment on, the review is no longer being imagined.

It is being written — one small impression at a time.

8 The Space Confirm the Yes

Arrival doesn't end at the door.

The moment guests step inside, the space either confirms everything they already believe — or quietly introduces doubt. This is where reassurance becomes real, and where the foundation for the review is laid, often before a single night has passed.

Preparedness is not about perfection.

It is about intention.

Guests notice immediately whether a space feels activated or dormant. A room that feels awake — lights on, air moving, temperature comfortable — signals readiness. It tells guests that someone was thinking about their arrival, not just the reservation.

This matters more than hosts often realize.

When guests feel welcomed early, they become more generous observers later. Small inconveniences are interpreted as accidents, not failures. Problems feel solvable rather than symbolic. The emotional tone set at arrival carries forward into how the entire stay is judged — and eventually described.

Preparedness creates that tone.

Small details do disproportionate work here.

A welcome guide that carries the same visual language guests have already encountered.

A brief message on the TV with the guest's name.

A logo they recognize — not as branding, but as continuity.

These elements don't impress.

They orient.

They quietly say, *"You're in the right place, and this was prepared for you."*

Comfort plays a role as well.

Air conditioning already set. Lights on. Curtains positioned intentionally. Guests shouldn't have to activate the space before settling into it. The fewer adjustments required in the first minutes, the more the space feels ready rather than reactive.

Cleanliness, here, goes beyond standard.

A clean space communicates care, not compliance. It suggests that preparation happened recently and specifically. Guests rarely comment on cleanliness when it's done well — but it becomes the baseline against which everything else is measured.

Preparedness also makes room for generosity.

A home-baked item.

Fruit from the garden.

Fresh flowers picked the same day.

These gestures are not about value.

They are about attention.

They slow guests down, interrupt the mechanics of arrival, and create a brief moment of receiving rather than managing.

This moment matters.

It often becomes the first emotional imprint of the stay — and the one guests return to mentally if something later doesn't go exactly as planned.

This is also where personal check-in, when offered, becomes powerful.

Not as a tour.

Not as a presentation.

But as presence.

A calm greeting. A few orienting words. An offer of help — followed by space. When guests meet the host, even briefly, trust becomes human. The stay no longer feels anonymous. And if something goes wrong later, communication becomes easier, more direct, and more forgiving.

Guests are more willing to reach out.

Hosts are more easily believed.

Solutions feel collaborative instead of corrective.

A full tour is rarely necessary.

In some cases, it can even overwhelm. Guests don't need to be shown everything. They need to know help is available and boundaries are respected. A few cues are enough. The space should speak for itself.

When preparedness, welcome, and presence align, the stay begins with goodwill.

And goodwill is the strongest buffer a host can have.

It shapes how guests interpret small issues.

It influences what they remember.

It determines the tone of the review long before it is written.

By the time guests leave, they rarely recount individual details. They describe how the stay felt. And that feeling was often set in the first minutes — when the space confirmed the choice they had already made.

9 Presence Without Pressure

Once guests have arrived and settled, the host's role changes.

The work of reassurance is mostly done. The space has confirmed the choice. The stay has begun. From here on, what matters is not how much the host communicates — but how presence is felt without becoming intrusive.

Guests want to know that help exists.

They do not want to feel monitored.

The difference between the two is subtle. It has less to do with frequency than with tone. Presence feels supportive when it is offered lightly — and withdrawn quickly.

This is why the first check-in after arrival matters.

A short message on the morning after the first night does quiet but important work. It signals attentiveness without demanding response. It creates an opening without forcing conversation. And it establishes that communication is easy — not conditional.

A message like this illustrates the point:

Good morning,

I hope you had a wonderful first night and are settling in well. Just checking in to see if everything is going smoothly and if there's anything you might need. We're always just a message away if you need anything.

All the best

This message does not ask for confirmation.

It does not introduce new information.

It does not require action.

It simply places the host within reach.

Most guests read it and respond briefly — often with reassurance of their own. A simple *"Everything is perfect, thank you for checking in"* reinforces the emotional balance of the stay. The exchange closes itself naturally.

Some guests don't read it at all.

And yet, the message still works.

When something later comes up and the guest realizes they missed the check-in message, the tone of the conversation often shifts immediately. The guest apologizes for not responding earlier. The issue is framed differently — not as a complaint, but as a continuation of an already considerate exchange.

This matters more than it appears.

By reaching out first, the host establishes goodwill before anything goes wrong. If an issue arises later, the guest is already speaking to someone who has demonstrated care. Communication becomes collaborative instead of corrective.

Presence prevents escalation.

This kind of check-in also allows silence to remain comfortable.

Guests who need nothing feel no pressure to respond. Guests who do need something feel invited — not like they're interrupting. The host remains present without occupying space.

That balance is what most guests respond to best.

Availability does not mean constant contact.

Repeated messages, unnecessary follow-ups, or reminders can quickly feel like supervision. Even friendly communication can create pressure when it asks guests to respond without reason. The most effective hosts understand that restraint is part of hospitality.

This becomes especially important when something goes wrong.

No stay is perfect. What guests remember is not whether a problem existed, but how safe it felt to mention it — and how calmly it was handled. A host who has already established presence without pressure is easier to trust in moments of friction.

Guests rarely expect perfection.

They do expect to be taken seriously.

As the stay continues, good hosting becomes less visible.

Guests stop noticing the host's role entirely. They move freely, confident that help is available if needed. This absence of friction is not accidental — it is the result of intentional restraint.

And when the stay comes to an end, that restraint shows up again.

Guests remember how the stay felt. They remember ease, responsiveness, and calm. Even small imperfections are interpreted more generously when communication never felt heavy.

Presence without pressure is not about doing less.

It is about knowing when to reach out — and when to step back.

And that judgment, more than any checklist, is what carries a stay smoothly toward a positive review.

10 When Something Goes Wrong

Not because the stay was poorly prepared, and not because the host failed. It happens because hosting involves real spaces, real people, and real time. A light stops working. An appliance behaves unexpectedly. Weather interferes. A misunderstanding surfaces.

What guests remember is not the absence of problems.

It's how safe it felt to address them.

By the time an issue arises, much of the outcome has already been decided.

Guests who arrived feeling welcomed, oriented, and supported approach problems differently than guests who arrived uncertain. They assume good intent. They expect cooperation. The tone of the stay has already shaped the tone of the conversation.

This is why the earlier chapters matter here.

When communication has been calm, timely, and optional — when presence was established without pressure — guests don't hesitate to reach out. And when they do, the message rarely feels accusatory. It feels practical.

The host's response at this moment matters more than the solution itself.

Speed helps, but tone decides. A calm acknowledgment reassures more than a rushed apology. Guests don't need dramatization. They need to know they've been heard and that the issue is being handled competently.

Defensiveness is the fastest way to escalate tension.

Explaining why something happened before acknowledging that it matters to the guest often sounds like dismissal — even when it isn't intended. The order matters:

Recognition first.

Action second.

Explanation, if needed, last.

Guests rarely expect perfection.

They do expect responsibility.

This is where trust either deepens or collapses.

When hosts respond with clarity and ownership, problems often become moments of reassurance rather than disappointment. Guests feel taken seriously. The experience feels human. Even inconvenient situations are reframed as temporary instead of symbolic.

Many hosts underestimate how forgiving guests can be.

A small issue handled well often strengthens the relationship. Guests appreciate transparency. They appreciate effort. They appreciate being included rather than managed.

This doesn't require over-communication.

Updates should be purposeful. Guests want to know what's happening — not to follow every step. Too much information can create anxiety. Just enough information restores confidence.

Resolution, when it comes, should feel complete.

Whether the fix is immediate or delayed, guests should feel that the issue has reached a clear endpoint. Loose ends leave mental residue. Closure restores ease.

Reviews reflect this.

Guests rarely describe issues in isolation. They describe how situations were handled. Phrases like "the host was responsive" or "they took care of it right away" carry more weight than a list of amenities.

This is the paradox of hosting.

Perfection is fragile.

Competence is durable.

When something goes wrong — and it will — the goal is not to defend the experience, but to protect the relationship. The trust built earlier gives you room to act calmly. And that calm, more than any fix, is what guests remember.

Not because nothing went wrong —

but because what mattered was handled with care.

11 Departure Is Part of the Stay

The stay does not end when the door closes.

It ends when the experience settles into memory. And that happens not during the final night, but in the moments surrounding departure — when guests transition from being present to reflecting on what just happened.

This is why departure matters more than hosts often realize.

By the time guests are preparing to leave, most of the experience has already been judged emotionally. What remains is not evaluation, but consolidation. Small gestures here don't change the stay — they shape how it is remembered.

Silence at departure can feel abrupt.

Not wrong, but unfinished. Guests don't need extended communication at this stage, but they do benefit from one final signal that the host remains attentive. A brief message on the morning of departure can do this quietly. But when possible, a personal goodbye does something more.

Stopping by briefly to say goodbye is not about procedure.

It's about presence.

A simple line — *"I just wanted to take a moment to personally say goodbye and wish you a safe journey"* — carries weight. Guests notice when a host shows up in person. It signals that their stay mattered enough to deserve time, not just messages.

This moment doesn't need structure.

It works best when it's natural. A short conversation. A genuine question. A shared laugh. These exchanges often surface the moments that mattered most to the guest — without prompting.

How was the waterfall you visited?

Did you end up enjoying the jacuzzi in the evenings?

How did the pool feel during the day?

These questions aren't about gathering feedback. They help guests replay their own experience. And what guests replay is what they later remember.

This is how memory is shaped — not by instruction, but by reflection.

A personal goodbye also changes the tone of everything that follows.

When guests have spoken with the host face to face, communication becomes warmer. If something small was imperfect, it feels easier to forgive. If something was especially meaningful, it feels easier to mention.

This moment also creates space for something else — a quiet, respectful acknowledgment of the role reviews play.

Not a request.

Not a reminder.

But context.

A brief line is enough: *"Reviews really matter to hosts like us — they help future guests know what to expect."* Said calmly, without urgency, this doesn't create pressure. It creates understanding.

Guests don't feel obligated.

They feel informed.

And when the time comes to follow up later with a written review request, it no longer feels transactional. It feels like a continuation of a conversation that already happened.

A personal goodbye is not always possible.

When it isn't, the same principles apply in writing. The tone should remain light. Appreciative. Complete. The goal is not to extract something from the guest, but to close the experience with care.

Departure is not the moment to add instructions.

Guests are already leaving. Their attention is shifting. Anything that feels corrective or procedural risks overshadowing what came before.

What guests carry with them is feeling.

Whether they felt noticed.

Whether the ending felt rushed or thoughtful.

Whether the stay felt like a transaction or a shared moment in time.

When departure is handled with presence — especially in person — the experience feels whole. Guests don't feel like they're exiting a process. They feel like they're leaving a place where they were welcomed, remembered, and appreciated.

And that feeling travels with them.

Long after the door has closed.

12 Closing the Loop

On Airbnb, the review does not happen whenever the guest feels like it.

It opens at a specific moment — typically in the afternoon after checkout — and both guest and host are notified at the same time. This timing is intentional. It creates a short pause after departure, then invites reflection while the stay is still fresh.

By the time that window opens, the experience is already complete.

What happens next is not about persuasion.

It is about how the stay is closed.

Many thoughtful hosts prepare for this moment in advance.

They already know what they will say about the guest — not because they are rushing to post, but because the stay has been observed carefully. When the review window opens, the host is ready to respond calmly, confidently, and without hesitation.

Posting the review early does quiet work.

It signals appreciation.

It establishes goodwill.

It sets a tone of generosity rather than delay.

Once the host's review is submitted, a natural opening appears.

This is where closing the loop becomes personal.

A short message sent after posting the review does not feel like a request. It feels like a continuation. A thank-you. A brief reference to something the guest enjoyed. And a simple note that a kind review has already been left.

Language here matters.

Not formal.

Not scripted.

Not transactional.

A message like this captures the tone:

"Thank you again for staying with us — it was a pleasure hosting you. I just wanted to let you know that I've left you a very nice review. If you have a moment, we'd truly appreciate one as well. I hope you arrived home safely."

This message does three things at once.

It expresses gratitude.

It personalizes the memory of the stay.

And it invites reciprocity without pressure.

Guests don't experience this as manipulation.

They experience it as fairness.

The review no longer feels like an abstract task. It feels like a response to something already offered. And because the host's tone has been consistent throughout the stay — calm, attentive, respectful — the guest's response tends to mirror it.

This moment is shaped by everything that came before.

Guests who felt welcomed on arrival, supported without pressure during the stay, and acknowledged at departure approach reviews differently. They are not deciding *whether* to leave one. They are deciding *how* to describe what they felt.

When a guest remembers a specific moment — a place they visited, a space they enjoyed, a detail that stood out — and hears it echoed back by the host, memory solidifies. The stay becomes a story rather than a list of features.

That story is what gets written.

Reviews that emerge this way feel fuller. More human. Less guarded. Even when a stay wasn't flawless, the tone remains generous because the relationship felt balanced.

Importantly, this approach respects choice.

There is no urgency.

No repeated reminders.

No pressure to perform.

If a guest chooses not to respond, the loop still closes cleanly. Appreciation has already been expressed. The experience ends with dignity.

But more often than not, guests respond.

Not because they were asked —

but because the exchange felt complete.

This is how reviews work when they are treated as reflections, not favors.

The host speaks first, with care.

The guest responds in kind.

And the final impression of the stay becomes one of mutual respect —

which is exactly what future guests will read.

Consistency Is What Remains

Short stays create long memories.

A guest may stay for two nights or a week, but the impression they carry lasts far longer. Over time, those impressions accumulate — not just in reviews, but in reputation. And reputation, unlike a single stay, is built slowly, through repetition.

Not repetition of features.

Repetition of feeling.

This is what long-term hosting rests on.

Guests don't remember every detail. They remember whether the experience felt easy. Whether communication felt human. Whether arrival felt prepared and departure felt complete. They remember whether everything they encountered — messages, tone, space, and presence — felt like it belonged together.

They remember consistency.

That consistency cannot be manufactured.

It has to come from somewhere real.

The most effective hosts are not those who adopt a "hosting voice," but those whose tone naturally reflects who they are and what their place represents. The personality of the property is never separate from the personality of the host. Even the most thoughtfully designed space is, in some way, a mirror.

When hosts enjoy hosting, that enjoyment shows up everywhere.

In how they write.

In how they respond.

In how they prepare the space.

In how they handle problems.

In how they say goodbye.

When that care is genuine, guests feel it immediately. And when it's forced or borrowed, they feel that too.

Consistency, then, is not about polish.

It's about honesty.

The tone of the listing, the language of the messages, the way arrival is handled, the rhythm of the stay — all of it should feel like expressions of the same person and the same place. Nothing needs to be exaggerated. Nothing needs to be performed. The goal is not to impress, but to remain recognizable.

Over time, that recognition compounds.

Reviews begin to echo one another. Words repeat themselves without being prompted. Calm. Thoughtful. Easy. Exactly as described. These patterns don't happen by accident. They emerge when guests encounter the same tone, again and again, across every moment of the journey.

This is where structure becomes supportive.

As hosting grows more complex — across platforms, messages, maps, and external touchpoints — maintaining that consistency becomes harder to do intuitively. Not because the host changes, but because the number of places where tone must live increases.

A website gives that consistency a fixed center — one place where tone lives intact, regardless of platform or moment.

It does not replace the listing.

It does not compete with the platform.

It quietly reinforces what guests already believe.

This understanding didn't come from theory.

It comes from a lifetime in hospitality — from working within large hotel organizations like Hyatt and Hilton, to smaller boutique restaurants and experiences, and now into the vacation rental world. Across all of these environments, the pattern remains the same: guests respond most strongly to coherence. When everything feels aligned, trust forms naturally.

The work continues.

Hosting evolves. Platforms change. Guest expectations shift. What remains constant is the need for experiences that feel honest, steady, and human.

That ongoing observation became the foundation for Visible PR — not as a branding exercise, but as a practical way to help hosts protect what already works. To translate lived hospitality experience into structures that make consistency easier to maintain over time.

This is not a finished system.

It's an ongoing study.

But the conclusion remains clear.

Hosts who protect consistency don't host louder.

They host steadier.

They don't chase improvement endlessly.

They reinforce what already feels right.

And that is what guests remember.

That is what reviews reflect.

And that is what lasts.

Afterword

From the Inside

I didn't set out to write a book.

This work grew slowly, alongside the act of hosting itself — through repetition, attention, and time. By noticing which stays felt easy, which conversations resolved themselves naturally, and which moments quietly shaped the experience without ever being discussed.

Those observations accumulated.

Not as a method.

Not as a system.

But as understanding.

I've spent my life in hospitality — from large hotel environments where consistency is engineered at scale, to smaller, more personal spaces where consistency lives in people rather than processes. Over time, I began to see that the most meaningful guest experiences weren't created by effort alone, but by alignment. When tone, intention, and delivery matched, things settled. When they didn't, even small details became heavier.

This book is simply a record of that noticing.

It doesn't ask hosts to become someone else.

It doesn't ask them to perform.

It asks them to pay attention to what already works — and protect it.

Along the way, I built structures to support that protection. Not because hosting needed more tools, but because consistency becomes harder to carry as complexity grows. Those structures eventually became the foundation of my work with Visible PR — not as an offering to sell, but as a way to help hosts preserve clarity as their presence expands.

What matters most, though, is not the structure.

It's the care behind it.

If this book has done its job, it hasn't told you what to do. It has helped you recognize moments you already understand — when a stay feels calm, when communication feels easy, when guests arrive aligned and leave appreciative.

From there, the path forward tends to reveal itself.

Hosting doesn't need to become louder to improve.

It needs to become steadier.

And when that happens, the experience carries itself — naturally, consistently, and over time.

Made in the USA
Monee, IL
04 November 2026

67386983R00036